Fostering Financial Literacy

Literacy

Money Lessons for Kids

Table of Contents

Chapter 1. Introduction

Welcome to our engaging Special Report, "Fostering Financial Literacy: Money Lessons for Kids!" It's never too early to start the essential journey of learning about money, and this comprehensive guide is perfect for helping children of all ages venture along this path. Brightening future prospects, one dollar at a time, we delve into effective methods, interactive activities, real world examples and much more to make financial concepts fun and easy to grasp. Prepare your children for a secure and prosperous tomorrow while delivering empowering life lessons today. Buy our insightful report and let's paint the future rich with knowledge and financial independence!

Chapter 2. Laying Financial Foundations: Basics of Money

An understanding of the nature of money is the starting point for all financial learning. Before we can talk about budgeting, savings, and investments, it's critical to understand what money is, where it comes from, how it changes in value, and how we use it in our everyday lives.

2.1. What is Money?

Money, in its most basic sense, serves three key functions: it is a medium of exchange, a unit of account, and a store of value.

As a medium of exchange, money allows us to purchase goods and services. Without it, we would be forced to barter, exchanging goods or services directly, which would be complicated and inconvenient.

It is also a unit of account, providing us a common measure of the value of goods and services. Each item for sale in the market is priced in units of money, simplifying transactions.

Lastly, money acts as a store of value. If we don't use our money immediately, we store it in a safe place, such as a bank, and it retains its value for future use.

2.2. Origin of Money

Surprisingly, money as we know it today hasn't always existed. The concept of using something concrete to represent value developed gradually over centuries.

Initially, many societies functioned on a barter system, where people would swap goods directly. Over time, societies began to settle on a select few items that were commonly seen as valuable – for example, gold or silver, cattle, or even shells. These items were accepted as a medium of exchange.

Later, coinage emerged around 600 BC, and paper money first appeared in China during the Tang Dynasty. Over the centuries, the paper money concept spread throughout the world, and today, it coexists with electronic transactions and digital currencies in our complex financial systems.

2.3. How Money Changes Value

You might have heard adults talking about the cost of goods "back in their day." This highlights an important aspect of money: its purchasing power or value changes over time. It's essential to know why.

Two main factors affect the value of money: inflation and deflation.

Inflation happens when prices for goods and services increase, resulting in your money having less purchasing power. It's why your grandparents could buy a candy bar for a nickel, while today the same candy bar might cost a dollar.

Deflation, on the other hand, happens when prices decrease, making money more valuable. This is relatively rare compared to inflation but can be equally disruptive to an economy.

2.4. How We Use Money Every Day

Each day, we participate in the economic cycle through transactions using money. Our activities can be generally classified into earning, spending, and saving/investing.

Earning involves performing a job or providing a service in exchange for money. Kids can experience this through activities like doing chores for an allowance, selling lemonade, or mowing neighbors' lawns.

Spending is the act of using money to buy goods and services. The reality of limited money supply makes budgeting a necessary skill, helping balance wants with needs.

Saving and investing is where you keep some money secure for future use. It could be as simple as saving for a new toy or more advanced concepts like banking and investments.

2.5. Opening a Bank Account

A great first step toward understanding the practical side of money is opening a bank account. While you may need a parent's guidance to set it up, managing your own savings and checking account can be extremely educational. This activity introduces children to banking norms, the concept of interest, bank statements and how to use an ATM.

2.6. Understanding Interest

Interest is an important concept in the world of banking and finance. Simply put, it's the cost of using someone else's money. When you save money in your bank account, the bank pays you to use your money – that's called interest on savings. When you borrow money, you pay the bank for using their money - that's called interest on borrowing.

Learning about interest early helps children understand that money can "grow" over time if saved or invested wisely. At the same time, borrowing money has a cost which needs to be carefully considered.

By understanding these basics about money and how it works, children can begin to form a basis for making sound financial decisions. As they grow and take on more financial responsibility, their future selves will thank them for the financier they nurtured today.

Chapter 3. Coins and Notes: Understanding the Value

Understanding the value and significance of coins and notes is the bedrock of financial literacy. As such, it's crucial to make sure children are well-versed in recognizing different denominations and understand their varying worth. Through a mixture of theory, practical activities, and real-world applications, this section will guide kids in grasping the basics of coins and notes.

3.1. Exploring Different Types of Money

Let's dip our toes into the world money! Here's a quick breakdown of currencies you'll find in the United States:

- Penny: 1 cent
- Nickel: 5 cents
- Dime: 10 cents
- Quarter: 25 cents
- Dollar Bill: 1 dollar
- Five Dollar Bill: 5 dollars
- Ten Dollar Bill: 10 dollars
- Twenty Dollar Bill: 20 dollars
- Fifty Dollar Bill: 50 dollars
- Hundred Dollar Bill: 100 dollars

When considering the rest of the world, the types of coins and notes can vary greatly. In the United Kingdom, for example, you'd find coins denominated in pence and pound sterling and notes in pounds.

3.2. Understanding Sizes and Physical Characteristics

Pay close attention to the coins and notes' physical characteristics, as size isn't always directly proportional to their value. For instance, a dime is smaller than a nickel but holds twice the value! Each coin is distinct in color, size, thickness, and design and serves as the populace's medium of exchange. This visual diversity among coins and banknotes aids in their easy identification and adds to their essence and character. A great way to practice this is to collect various denominations and engage in a sorting activity based on their physical attributes and values.

3.3. Assigning Value to Coins and Notes

An essential step when it comes to financial literacy is learning to assign the correct value to different coins and notes. Start by introducing the concept of 'value' focusing on the lowest denomination – a penny. Explain that a penny carries a worth of one cent. Four quarters make a dollar, and so on. Use visual aids and charts to make this process engaging and effective:

Coin/Note	Value
Penny	1 cent
Nickel	5 cents
Dime	10 cents
Quarter	25 cents
One Dollar Bill	1 dollar
Five Dollar Bill	5 dollars
Ten Dollar Bill	10 dollars
Twenty Dollar Bill	20 dollars
Fifty Dollar Bill	50 Dollars
Hundred Dollar Bill	100 dollars

3.4. Fun Exercises to Enhance Understanding

Money lessons don't have to be mundane. Incorporate practical exercises like a mock-marketplace where children act as both, the buyer and the seller. These experiences foster understanding of how transactions work and the value of money. Flash card games featuring various denominations and shopping exercises using real or pretend money can also be extremely beneficial.

3.5. Money Mathematics: Addition and Subtraction

Applying basic arithmetic skills to money is a fun and practical means of developing competency in both mathematical thinking and financial acumen. Here, we emphasize the importance of understanding how to add and subtract different denominations in real-world scenarios. For instance, if you give a five-dollar note to pay for an item costing three dollars, you would get two dollars back.

3.6. Saving and Spending Wisely

Drill down to the importance of spending money wisely and saving for the future. It's essential to grasp that while coins and notes are used for purchasing, not every desire needs immediate fulfillment. Teaching budgeting at this stage can help children track their spending and form wise money habits early.

3.7. Wrapping Up: Real World Applications

After understanding the intricate details about coins and notes, it's time to take this knowledge to the streets. Visit a local grocery store or farmer's market and allow children to handle financial transactions. Exercises like these offer practical applications of the lessons learned and help further cement the understanding of different coins and notes' value.

With consistent practice and exploration, comprehending the value of coins and notes will become second nature to children. After mastering this chapter, they will be well-prepared to navigate the world of money with confidence and understanding. The next step on this financial literacy journey is learning about banks and their role in safeguarding our money, which we look at in the next chapter.

Remember, patience and practice are the keys to success. It's a journey that starts with baby steps towards a financially secure and prosperous future.

Chapter 4. Earnings, Spending, Saving: The Trio of Finance

Understanding the trio of finance - earnings, spending, and saving - is critical to developing sound financial habits. Comprehending this triad is an essential stepping stone towards achieving financial literacy and freedom for children and adults alike.

4.1. Earnings: The First Step to Financial Independence

Earning money occurs in many ways, starting with simple tasks in a child's world like household chores rewarded with an allowance, to adults working in various jobs and businesses. Understanding earnings means understanding the function of work and time investment. In real terms, one trades their time and expertise for money. This concept can be simplified for children by using relatable examples and activities. For instance, a lemonade stand signifies initial capital investment, effort and time, which finally gets translated into earnings when they successfully sell their product.

Interactive Activities to Understand Earnings:

- Set up a pretend store at home with pretend money, where kids can practice transactions.

- Provide opportunities for children to earn, e.g., doing house chores.

- Discuss various jobs with kids, talk about how people earn in different professions.

4.2. Spending: The Second Pillar of Finance

Spending is the direct usage of earnings to acquire goods or services. Teaching children how their choices today can affect their finances tomorrow is crucial in making them smart spenders. This lesson goes hand-in-hand with understanding the value of money and how one dollar spent now is one less dollar for the future. Discussing needs versus wants, cost-efficient buying, and the impacts of impulsive spending will enable children to wisely navigate their way around money.

Interactive Activities to Understand Spending:

- Play 'Needs and Wants' sorting game. Write down various items, and ask your kids to classify them into needs and wants.
- Plan a family budget for a pretend vacation, emphasizing values such as compromise and saving.
- Use games like 'Monopoly' to demonstrate cash flow and promote strategic spending.

4.3. Saving: The Final Yet Vital Piece of the Puzzle

Saving is the act of setting aside a portion of earnings for future use, which can either be for a specific goal or unexpected expenses. Learning to save helps kids understand delayed gratification and the importance of preparing for the future. Discuss how money can grow over time through interest and the power of compound interest. Financial tools such as savings accounts, piggy banks, or allowances can be fruitful teaching aids.

Interactive Activities to Understand Saving:

- Set up a save, spend, and share jars to foster saving habits.

- Assist kids in opening their first savings account, discussing why it's beneficial.

- Create a savings goal chart for a desired toy or game, promoting a visual understanding of progress.

4.4. Maintaining a Balance: Earning, Spending, and Saving in Unison

Now that we've unbundled earnings, spending, and saving, it's essential to know the significance of maintaining a balance among this trio. By encouraging your children to earn their pocket money, make informed decisions when spending it, and save a portion for their future, they will learn about budgeting. It's the collaboration of these three elements that helps to establish a secure financial foundation.

Interactive Activities to strike a Balance:

- Ask your children to create a weekly or monthly budget based on their allowance.

- Chart their spending habits over a period, enabling them to visualize where their money goes.

- Discuss the concept of 'Pay Yourself First,' teaching them to allocate a certain percentage to savings before spending.

Remember, introducing these core financial concepts will not always result in immediate understanding. Patience, clarity, and repetition will be your strongest allies in this endeavour. It's not just about teaching kids the mechanics of money but also empowering them with the values and habits that support sound financial decisions.

By laying the groundwork early, we enable our children to lead the charge towards financial autonomy, equipping them with the knowledge and skills they need to navigate the wide, and sometimes daunting, world of finance.

Chapter 5. Bank Accounts and Piggy Banks: Where Money Lives

One of the initial steps in teaching financial literacy to children is insightfully elucidating the concept of storing money. Billions of people around the globe keep their earnings secure in bank accounts, while our youngest savers often start by stashing their pennies in piggy banks. Going beyond these physical manifestations, the more profound lessons tied to these entities include understanding the value of money, the importance of saving, secure money handling, and myriad financial concepts that are sure to be fruitful in our everyday lives.

5.1. The Piggy Bank: Not Just A Toy

Teaching children about money starts at an impressively young age. One of the simplest and most recognizable financial education tools is the piggy bank. Yet, beyond being a cute ornament, it embodies the virtue of saving and provides an engaging way to introduce financial concepts to young minds.

Firstly, it's crucial to help kids understand why they should save money. Explain that money is limited and should be grown and guarded for current needs and future desires. This step plays a prominent role in teaching delayed gratification—having the patience to save up for a bigger, better reward instead of spending instantly on small, fleeting pleasures.

Children as young as three years old can commence their saving regime with a piggy bank. Let your child pick out their own, turning the exercise into a fun ritual. They'll be more compelled to save if their piggy bank is appealing to their tastes. Encourage them to add spare coins and any cash gifts they receive. And remember, reference is key! Make sure to consistently emphasize that the money being saved is for future use.

It's necessary to occasionally count the coins together and write down the totals to track progress. This activity not only teaches the importance of record-keeping but also helps kids improve basic addition and subtraction skills. Furthermore, it makes children eager to see how their savings grow over time, nurturing in them an awareness and appreciation for the gradual growth of savings—a pace distinct from the instantaneity they're used to in our fast-paced world.

Meet their incremental savings with praise and support, reinforcing the importance of saving and fostering a meaningful connection between them and their piggy banks.

5.2. Transitioning to Bank Account: From Boxes to Banks

As your child reaches the teenage years, they might start to outgrow their piggy bank. That's the perfect time to introduce a safer, more sophisticated method of saving - the bank account. Just as you transitioned them from a tricycle to a bicycle, it's time you transitioned them from piggy banks to bank accounts.

Tell them about a bank's function, its role within the economic system, and why people put their money there. Explain the security measures undertaken by banks to protect their deposits: vaults, round-the-clock surveillance, and government insurance. Emphasize that while their money is secure in the bank, it also has the ability to grow through interest accumulation, further instilling the culture of saving.

The next step is to open a student savings account for your teenager.

Many banks offer these types of accounts, which often come with attractive benefits such as lower fees and higher interest rates. Compared to regular bank accounts, they have simpler requirements for opening, making them the perfect conduit to bank interactions for teens.

Teenagers should be actively involved in the bank account creation process, so they get comfortable dealing with banking procedures. Let them fill out the forms, speak with bank officials, and manage the account themselves.

One crucial point to highlight while interacting with banks is online safety. As we march towards a digital future, your child needs to learn about the risks of online transactions, including fraud and identity theft. Teach them never to share personal details online, even if prompted by someone claiming to be a bank official.

Moving forward, make sure you review the bank statement with your children every month. This experience not only provides practical insight into transactions, account balances, and banking operations but also encourages dialogue about personal finance handling.

5.3. Savings Furthered: Understanding Interest

One major leap from piggy banks to banks is the concept of interest. Introduce your child to this integral financial idea which promotes saving by giving a reward. Explain how banks pay them a small amount, known as interest, for keeping their money safe. It's essentially earning money from saved money.

To help this notion sink in, you can create an incentive-based model at home. For instance, add an extra 10% to their savings at the end of every month. If they saved $50 in January, in February they will have

$55. Here you act as the bank, and the extra $5 is interest. This visual demonstration will endow them with a better understanding of how interest works.

5.4. What's Next? Introduction To Investments

After mastering the basics of savings and interest, your child is ready to sail ahead towards the concept of investments. Reinforce the idea that money isn't just for immediate spending or saving for future expenditure. It can - and should - be used strategically to make more money or to support causes they believe in.

Investments are essentially buying assets you expect to increase in value over time or that provide a return in the form of interest or dividends. This can be in the form of stocks, bonds, Mutual funds, or other types of assets. While the details will need simplification when talking to children, the basic principle is key: investments can let money work for you.

However, ensure that they understand that investments carry risks, unlike bank accounts. The value of investments can go up, but it may also go down, sometimes significantly. In essence, it's crucial for them to comprehend that greater potential rewards often come with a higher risk quotient.

Let's continue fostering financial literacy, and our children will step into the world empowered with knowledge and wisdom about money. It will strengthen them not only with the capability to make better financial decisions, but also promote responsible behavior that will ripple throughout their lives. Remember, wise financial habits cultivated during childhood often become the foundation of a sound economic understanding in adulthood, enabling a bright future rich with knowledge and financial independence.

We will delve into further financial empowerment concepts in the forthcoming sections. Stay tuned to equip your child with the essential proficiency of navigating through the intricate world of finances, painting the future thriving with financial wisdom.

Chapter 6. Lemonade Stands and More: Lessons on Entrepreneurship

Encouraging entrepreneurship among children is an incredible way to introduce them to monetary responsibility and business acumen from a young age. One of the most classic real-world experiences that can illuminate this path is the traditional lemonade stand. This seemingly simple enterprise can provide abundant lessons on the essentials of entrepreneurship, including planning, budgeting, marketing, customer service, and even tax basics.

6.1. Planning the Lemonade Stand

A successful lemonade stand begins with planning. Pressing the lemons and adding the sugar doesn't create a business alone – a degree of foresight and organization is necessary.

First, a decision needs to be made on where to set up the stand. Since location plays a crucial role in business, help your child understand how selecting a high-traffic area can increase chances of visibility and making sales.

Next is deciding on the product. Lemonade is traditional, but your child could consider offering other drinks or snacks to diversify the range. Supply and demand is a practical concept here. How many potential customers are there? Are there other lemonade stands in the neighborhood offering competition?

A comprehensive plan also includes things like deciding on operating hours, organizing supplies, determining how to present the stand, and much more.

6.2. Budgeting and Pricing Strategy

Budgeting is another fundamental aspect of running a lemonade stand. Guide your child through estimating the total costs of running the stand – including raw materials (lemons, sugar, water, cups), stand setup costs, and even your time. Teach them to differentiate between fixed costs (like the table and a sign) and variable costs (like lemons and cups) and why they are important in the budget planning.

Next, help them decide on pricing. They'll need to price their lemonade in a way that covers costs and still provides profit. This pricing lesson introduces the concept of 'return on investment,' or ROI, a key financial term.

6.3. Marketing and Advertising Your Business

No business can succeed without attracting customers, making marketing and advertising essential elements of the entrepreneurial mix. Kids can get creative with colorful signs, catchy slogans, or even offering free samples to attract a crowd.

This experience can teach them about the importance of an attractive product presentation, customer engagement, promotional strategies, and the effects of word-of-mouth endorsements.

6.4. Providing Excellent Customer Service

Your child's interaction with customers at the lemonade stand is an early lesson in customer service. Teach them about polite communication, maintaining a cheerful attitude, handling complaints or unsatisfied customers, and the value of building customer loyalty.

6.5. Understanding Tax Basics

Although kids are too young to file taxes, a lemonade stand is a great place to start understanding this concept. Talk to them about how, in a real business, a portion of the earnings goes to the government as income tax.

Mention the importance of receipts and keeping track of earnings and expenses, which will be the groundwork for learning about financial documentation and accountability in the future.

6.6. From Lemonade Stands to Future Ventures

The experience with the lemonade stand prepares kids for future business ventures. Discuss with them how the skills they have learned can be applied to other businesses, whether it's a car-washing service, lawn mowing venture, or even a tech startup.

Also, talk to them about the concept of scaling and expansion, and saving up profits to re-invest in the business. Mention success stories of young entrepreneurs for inspiration.

In conclusion, a lemonade stand provides practical business and economic principles in an inviting, fun, and age-appropriate way. While the stand might appear to be a simple, summertime activity, with the right approach, it can become a catalyst for building financial literacy and entrepreneurial skills. These early lessons will help kids view money as a tool rather than just a means to an end, giving them a head start in their financial future.

Chapter 7. Budgeting for Beginners: Guiding Spending Habits

Understanding the concept of budgeting is the first crucial step towards financial literacy. It forms the solid foundation of sound spending habits. In essence, budgeting is about balancing your income with your expenses. It enables you to prioritize your spending to ensure that the crucial areas of your life are sufficiently catered for.

7.1. Setting the Scene

For children embarking on the financial journey, creating and managing a budget may seem like an enormous task. Yet, it's a vital life skill integral to their future financial stability. Here we simplify it, by presenting relatable scenarios. Imagine, for example, having a set number of sweets. If you eat them all at once, you won't have any left for later. But if you make a plan – a budget – on how to distribute them, you might be able to enjoy the sweets longer. A budget for money works on the same principle – you divide your income – your 'sweets' – to last you a specific time while meeting your needs and wants.

7.2. Why Budget?

Budgeting is important because it helps you control your spending, save money, avoid debt, and prepare for emergencies. Think about a goal your child may have, such as buying a new toy, a bicycle, or saving for college. With a proper budget, that goal becomes achievable. It doesn't even stop at tangible things; budgeting also imparts a sense of financial discipline and responsibility that stays with them into adulthood.

7.3. Starting Simple

Start by teaching children to document their income and expenses. Include allowances, birthday money, and any earned money for the income. Expenses might be money spent on sweets, toys, or movies. Use a simple table format (asciidoc) for documentation.

Income	Expense	Balance
10	2	8
20	5	15

In the table above, Income is the money received, and Expense is where the money was spent. The Balance is what's left after the expense has been deducted from the income.

7.4. Accommodating Needs and Wants

Children must learn the difference between needs and wants as they can easily blur. Needs are things you cannot go without — like food and shelter. Wants, on the other hand, are the extras that enhance life — like toys or candy. Allocating a budget for both needs and wants helps achieve a balance. A good practice is to prioritize the needs before allocating the remaining income to the wants.

7.5. Allocating and Tracking Budget

Once there is an understanding of income, expense, needs, and wants, children can now start creating their own budgets. A good starting point is a 50/30/20 rule, where 50% of income goes to needs, 30% to wants, and 20% to savings. This way, they can track their expenditure and savings.

Again, a simple table (asciidoc markup) can help visualize the budget.

Category	Income %	Amount	Balance
Needs	50	10	10
Wants	30	6	4
Saving	20	4	0

In the table above, the income is divided into categories, and the specific Amount allocated to each category based on the percentages. Finally, the Balance is the money left after all allocations.

7.6. The Saving Game: Understanding Long-term Goals

Offer real-world scenarios that mimic saving for long-term goals. Suggest saving for a pricier toy or a special outing which will require time to save up for. Empower your child to make decisions about when to save and when to spend. Let them see that spending may bring instant gratification, but saving leads to reaching bigger goals. Reinforce this by applauding their small victories along the way.

7.7. Conclusion

Remember, the goal is to raise children who are financially smart and responsible. Although the journey may be challenging, achieving this goal is rewarding. By practicing budgeting at an early age, they'll grow and mature in understanding financing, thereby avoiding the potential pitfalls that come with money management in adulthood. Starting simple, acknowledging the difference between needs and wants, allotting wisely, and cherishing the power of saving are some of the lessons that children can carry with them forever.

Chapter 8. Investing for Kids: A Peak into the Future

Investing may seem complex at first, but is simply the process of putting your money in various platforms or ventures with an expectation of a profitable return. Let's take this journey to demystify investing for young minds, transforming seemingly convoluted concepts into straightforward, bite-sized lessons.

8.1. Understanding Investment

Investing for children may seem a remote idea, but one must understand that investing is not just about the financial gain. It's about understanding value and learning how to grow it. The principles of investing are not hard to learn. They revolve around simple concepts like taking calculated risks and understanding the value of patience.

In simplified terms, investing is like planting a seed and waiting for it to grow into a big tree. You carefully choose the seed (investment), give it what it needs to grow (time and money), and eventually, you'll have a tree that bears fruit (returns). Once children grasp this concept, they are already on their way to understanding the basic premise behind investments.

8.2. Starting with Savings

Before diving into the world of investments, it's important to stress the importance of savings. Indeed, savings form the springboard from which all future investments leap. Consider savings as an essential 'safety net'. Money saved can be divided into portions, part of which would be slated for investments. This should be the first step in our path to understanding investments.

For young minds to grasp this, consider this example. Suppose a child saves a part of their allowance each week. As the weeks turn into months, they will notice their little funds grow significantly in size. Here the child sees the concept of cumulative growth firsthand - a fundamental principle in the world of investing.

8.3. Understanding Risks and Returns

An investment comes with two important aspects: risks and returns. The phrase 'higher the risk, higher the return' often holds in the world of investments. Understanding this balance is crucial for any budding investor.

An engaging way of teaching this could be through the classic game of 'Snakes and Ladders.' In the game, a player can choose to take smaller steps with fewer risks (snakes) or choose ladders, which, while promising greater advancement (returns), also carry a risk of falling from high places (losses).

8.4. Learning About Diversification

Diversification, in the world of investments, refers to spreading investments across a variety of platforms to manage risks. It's the old adage of not putting all your eggs in one basket. For children, a real world example would be to compare investments to their favourite candies. If they buy only one kind and suddenly decide they don't like it anymore, they're stuck with it. But purchasing a mix of candies ensures they still have a variety to enjoy.

8.5. Recognizing the Power of Compound Interest

Albert Einstein famously said that compound interest is the eighth wonder of the world. This key concept in investing is another fundamental pillar.

Imagine your savings as a pet bunny. Now, bunnies are known for their prolific reproduction rates. So, in no time, your one bunny becomes four bunnies, then sixteen, and so on. In the same way, compound interest means your money grows exponentially over time - like your bunny family!

8.6. Investment Tools for Kids

There are several real-world financial products designed specifically for children that offer them a firsthand investing experience.

Begin with a simple savings account, then venture into certificates of deposit, and eventually explore junior ISAs and bonds tailored for children. Each of these tools offers a different level of risk, returns, and commitment, making them excellent models for learning investment principles.

8.7. Learning with Stock Market Games

Online stock market games are interactive tools that simulate the live stock market. These games offer a fun and risk-free platform for kids to apply investing principles, make trades, and understand market dynamics. It's like playing Monopoly, but on the actual market!

8.8. Ripple Effect of Early Investing

Starting the journey of investing early has effectiveness twofold. First, it acclimatizes children to think about their financial future from an early age, sowing the seeds of financial responsibility. Secondly, due to the magic of compound interest, the earlier you start, the bigger your potential returns will be.

In conclusion, the world of investing offers rich lessons on value, growth, patience, calculated risks, and smart strategies. By introducing children to these concepts early on, we're not just teaching them to handle money. We're equipping them with skills for life.

Chapter 9. Understanding Credit and Debt: The Power and Pitfalls

Getting to grips with the concepts of credit and debt is a key part of financial literacy, especially for kids who are preparing to make their way in a financially complex world. By understanding these pivotal financial tools, children can learn how to confidently navigate their future monetary decisions and responsibilities.

9.1. Understanding Credit

Let's start with credit. Credit is essentially borrowed money that you can use to purchase goods and services. However, this 'borrowed money' isn't free. When you use credit, you promise to pay back the money within a specific period, often with an additional amount known as interest.

The most common form of credit is a credit card. When you use a credit card, you actually borrow money from the credit card company to make your purchases. Every month, you're required to pay at least a portion of your balance. If you don't pay in full, the remaining balance accrues interest.

9.2. The Power of Credit

Credit has numerous advantages:

1. It allows for affordable large purchases: If we had to save up for every big purchase, it could take years. Credit enables us to buy expensive items like houses or cars before we've saved the total cost.

2. Emergency funds: It can serve as an emergency fund during an unexpected event such as a job loss or a significant expense.

3. Building Credit: Using credit wisely can help you establish a good credit history. This will be beneficial when applying for big loans in the future, including a mortgage for a house.

But remember, with great power comes great responsibility. Using credit requires self-discipline. It can be easy to spend beyond your means with credit, leading to a high interest-bearing debt.

9.3. Understanding Debt

Next, we move to the concept of debt. In the simplest terms, debt is money owed from one party to another. Typically, the borrower receives a certain amount of money (the debt), and is obligated to pay back the amount (the principal) along with any agreed-upon interest.

9.4. The Pitfalls of Debt

Debt itself is not harmful if it's managed properly. However, it becomes a problem when not handled correctly. Here are three main pitfalls to understand:

1. High Interest Rates: High-interest debts, like credit card debt, can add up to significant amounts if left unpaid.

2. Over-Borrowing: More amount of debt means more to repay, and if spending isn't controlled, it can lead to a cycle of debt which is tough to escape.

3. Poor Credit Score: Consistent failure to meet debt repayment commitments can lead to a poor credit score, which may impact the ability to borrow in the future.

9.5. How to Manage Debt

Now that we have a basic understanding of debt and its potential pitfalls, here's how to manage it:

1. Spend Wisely: Avoid unnecessary debts. This can be achieved through wise spending and saving habits.

2. Create a Budget: By creating and sticking to a budget, we can ensure we don't borrow more than we can repay.

3. Pay Debts on Time: Ensuring timely repayments not only avoids additional interest but also helps maintain a good credit score.

9.6. The Intersection of Credit and Debt

Credit and debt are two sides of the same coin. To use credit is to take on debt. Therefore, understanding how the two are interconnected is crucial:

1. Responsible Credit Use = Manageable Debt: Using credit responsibly can lead to manageable debt. For example, making purchases on credit but paying them off promptly prevents the debt from accumulating.

2. Overuse of Credit = Excessive Debt: Conversely, the overuse or misuse of credit can lead to overwhelming debt. High-interest debt from credit cards, for instance, can quickly add up if it's not punctually paid off.

Understanding and managing credit and debt is a fundamental component of financial literacy. By mastering these concepts, one can navigate the complexities of personal finance with confidence and build a stable financial future. The key is knowledge and discipline - when youngsters understand these principles and use them wisely, a secure financial future awaits!

Chapter 10. Charitable Giving: The Joy of Sharing Wealth

Understanding the essence of generosity and the impact of charitable giving is a crucial aspect of financial literacy. The pervasive question for many is not if to give, but rather, how? To teach children about financial stewardship and generosity, it's necessary to engage them in acts of giving that demonstrate the joy of sharing wealth.

10.1. The Benefits of Charitable Giving

Charitable giving opens a window to the world, fostering empathy and broader understanding. Children who are taught about philanthropy not only learn about money management but also about social responsibility.

In the process, they learn to recognize the imbalances and inequalities that permeate our society and how their contributions can provide relief to those in need. Childrens' financial education should provide: - An understanding of the significance and emotional rewards of giving. - The means to develop a personal philosophy about sharing and kindness.

Let's dive deeper into how you can guide your children in this direction.

10.2. Making Giving a Habit

Start by making charitable giving a habit in your house. For instance, during the holiday season, encourage your child to donate a portion of their pocket money or savings to a cause they care about.

Introduce the concept of 'Dividing The Dollar', where a dollar earned could be divided into three parts: 'spending', 'saving', and 'giving'. This simple division strategy establishes a bedrock for responsible financial behavior while fostering a lifelong habit of charity.

10.3. Interacting With Local Communities

Involving your child in charitable activities within local communities can offer hands-on experience in philanthropy. Not only does it enhance their understanding of their community's needs, but it also humbles them, teaching them gratitude for the resources they have.

Organize weekend visits to local charitable organizations where they can donate their time or resources. They can distribute food at soup kitchens, donate their old books to a community library, or plant trees in neighborhood parks.

10.4. Choosing a Cause That Resonates

Choosing a cause that resonates with your child can give their giving purpose. Encourage them to research various charitable organizations, understanding what each one stands for, and where their donations go.

This research will inspire them to find a cause they feel strongly about, be it animal welfare, climate change, poverty alleviation, or education. Financial gifts to these organizations are not just monetary transactions, but a child's compassionate contribution to a cause they care deeply about.

10.5. Monitoring the Impact

Irrespective of the amount, it's essential to teach children that every contribution matters. Organizations often send updates about how donations have been used, and this is a great way to show kids the real-life impact of their gesture. Evidence of the positive effects of their contribution can foster a sense of pride and satisfaction, reinforcing the joy of giving.

10.6. Engaging in Fundraising Activities

Fundraising provides an opportunity to tap into your child's creativity while also teaching them about financial responsibility. They could initiate a bake sale, a fun run, or a car wash with all proceeds going to their chosen charity. This offers a tangible encounter with the gift of giving and demonstrates how collective efforts can bring about significant results.

10.7. Talking About Money and Goals

Open discussions about money, including budgeting for charitable donations, instills a sense of accountability. The act of sharing wealth should be a conscious decision guided by sound financial planning.

Explain the importance of setting aside a defined amount for charity regularly, planning this into their monetary goals. These conversations can lay the foundation for good financial habits, paving the way for monetarily and socially responsible adults.

Teaching children the joy of sharing wealth is a layered process, woven with lessons of empathy, gratitude, financial planning, and generosity. By orienting them to the act of giving early, we are nurturing responsible, deeply aware citizens who are capable of contributing positively to their communities and society at large. Knowledge of the power of charitable giving is a wealth shared – a wealth that multiplies manifold when passed forward.

Let's create a generation mindful of their financial actions, balancing personal prosperity with societal welfare, and shaping a financially literate, empathetic and generous world.

Chapter 11. Prepping for Adulthood: Advanced Financial Concepts

Understanding finance is essential in today's ever-evolving economic landscape. As your children grow, they will need to face real-world economic challenges and make complex decisions related to savings, spending, and investing money. The right foundation will empower them not only to meet these challenges but to turn them into opportunities for financial wellness and prosperity. This section will introduce, explain, and simplify advanced financial concepts for your budding young adults.

11.1. Budgeting and Saving

At the heart of financial literacy is the concept of budgeting and saving. A budget is a plan for how to spend your money, whereas saving is the practice of setting aside a portion of your earnings for future use, emergencies or life goals.

Explain the importance of distinguishing between needs and wants. For example, food is a need, while fancy gadgets are wants. Understanding this difference is critical in making intelligent spending decisions. Furthermore, discuss the concept of emergency savings. An emergency fund is a safety net that can cover unexpected expenses, such as medical emergencies or sudden unemployment.

When illustrating these concepts to your children, using real-life situations can be extremely beneficial. Demonstrate various scenarios where budgeting and saving came in handy and how they aid in achieving life goals or combating unforeseen expenses.

11.2. Credit and Loans

As your children grow older, they will likely encounter situations where they will need to borrow money, whether for higher education, purchasing a house or starting a business. It's important to understand the way credit works, and how to manage debt responsibly.

Explain what a loan is and how it works - that it's money borrowed from a lender under the condition that it will be paid back in time, generally with interest. Discuss different types of loans, such as student loans, home mortgages, and auto loans, along with their respective terms and conditions.

Also, examine the concept of a credit score: a numerical expression of a person's creditworthiness, which can affect their ability to lease an apartment, secure a loan, or even get a job.

11.3. Investing and Compound Interest

To really grow wealth, it's integral to introduce the concept of investing. Investing involves committing money in order to earn a financial return. This essentially means that instead of keeping all of your money in a savings account, you put some of it in places where it can earn more money for you.

Take this opportunity to explore different types of investments such as stocks, bonds, and real estate, discussing the potential risks and rewards associated with each.

Then, delve into the concept of compound interest, sometimes referred to as "interest on interest". Unlike simple interest, which only grows in direct proportion to the initial investment, compound interest grows exponentially, offering far more potential for wealth accumulation over time.

11.4. Real Estate and Mortgages

The concept of real estate and mortgages is an essential part of financial literacy. This field can be complex, so begin with the basics. Introduce real estate as a physical property that includes land and buildings. Then, explain that people often buy real estate with the help of a loan known as a mortgage.

Ensure your children understand the concept of mortgages: a type of loan specifically designed to purchase buildings or land. Discuss how mortgages are paid back over time and explain the implications of failing to make repayments on time.

11.5. Financial Risks and Insurance

Lastly, discuss the concept of risk. Risk comes with nearly every financial decision we make. Understanding risks and how to manage them is an essential skill.

Talk about insurance as a tool for managing risk. By paying a relatively small amount of money regularly, we can protect ourselves against financially devastating events like a serious accident or illness, property damage, or theft.

Our modern financial system offers a diverse array of options and complexities. As your children become adults, they will face increasingly complex financial decisions. By preparing them with an understanding of these advanced financial concepts, you are setting them up to make informed decisions and promoting their financial independence and prosperity.